The Dog That Taught Me Tennis

Sally Huss

The Dog That Taught Me Tennis

Copyright © 2016 Sally Huss Inc./Huss Publishing
All rights reserved.
ISBN: 1945742100
ISBN: 13: 9781945742101

The Dog That Taught Me Tennis

    I have played tennis for many years and still do, and have played it quite well if you are keeping score. But, it was not until I met Gracie that I really learned the game.

    Gracie is a Blue Heeler, a very serious dog, with the over-riding intention of always keeping things in order. She likes to herd people, kids and adults alike. It is her nature, as she was bred to herd cattle, nipping at their heels to keep them in line and in a pack.

When I met Gracie her herding days were nearly over, but her tennis days were just getting under way. She had been adopted by my neighbor, a fellow children's book author, Ashley Birtwell.

To get acquainted, we three went for a walk to the nearby park. Ashley pulled out a tennis ball and Gracie was in heaven. Ashley threw it and Gracie retrieved it… again and again. Tennis ball dogs never stop; Gracie was one of them. I could see that Ashley had a limited range in her throwing.

So the next time we went out, I brought my tennis racket to knock the ball a good bit further. Gracie was delighted.

It was on the way back from one of these outings that Gracie revealed her genuine champion nature.

We decided to introduce her to my husband Marv, a former champion athlete himself in basketball and baseball with a fairly good ability in tennis. This was long ago. Now, he is a champion Tweeter, each day sending out inspirational messages that he culls from my King Features syndicated panel *Happy Musings*. He intersperses these wonderful thoughts with mentions of our children's books and occasionally promotes one of my tennis books as well.

Between his Tweeting sessions, it was Marv's habit to stretch his back out on a lovely blue couch in the living room area and watch the news. That's where he met Gracie.

She walked in with a tennis ball in her mouth

and demanded action. She must have sensed that Marv had been a pitcher.

He sat up, took the ball from her mouth and chucked it up in the air. Without a bit of hesitation, Gracie jumped up and caught it.

Then it began, one ball after the other, Marv tossing and Gracie Jumping. I went about my business

fixing dinner and could hear the commotion in the background. Marv would say to me, "Look at this. She never misses." I would take a peek. Yes, she seemed to never miss the ball, no matter how high Marv would toss it.

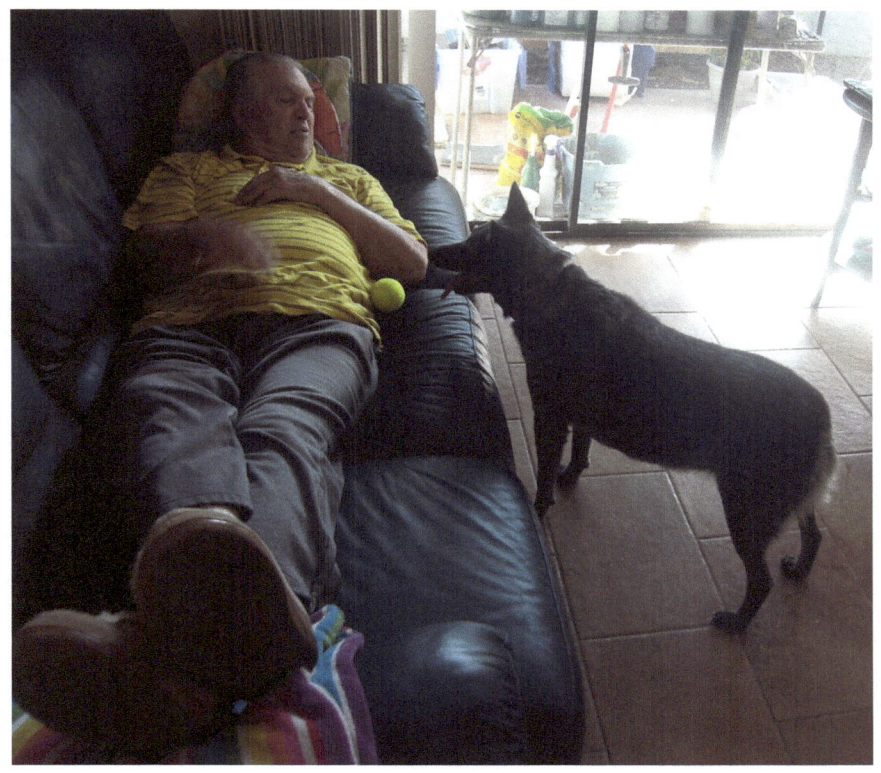

After about twenty minutes into this game, Gracie's true colors began to show. Marv was tiring and lay back down on the couch. Gracie was not tired and had come to play.

That's when I came in, sat down, and studied my new coach. This is what I discovered:

PERFECT FOCUS – HOW TO HAVE IT

Gracie had nothing else on her mind except playing ball. She focused on the ball exclusively. She lived for it to be in action so that she could act.

How many times on a tennis court do we players have perfect focus? How many times have we missed a ball then said to ourselves, *I didn't look at it*? It is one of the key ingredients of great champions – the ability to channel the mind in one direction, on one thing and not scatter one's attention to all sorts of extraneous happenings.

The secret to focus is one thing and Gracie had it – love. Gracie loved to jump and catch that ball. Nothing was more important to her than the ball. We would put a bowl of water down for her, even a bowl of food and she could not be swayed. The ball was number one in her life at that moment. And, to a dog, there is no other moment, only NOW. Gracie was present totally in the NOW through the very thing we all value most – love.

Some players say they love tennis and in part they do, but perhaps not as much as Gracie.

NON-JUDGMENTAL ATTITUDE – WHY IT'S USEFUL

Because we are thinking beings, as opposed to Gracie who is an instinctual being, our minds cannot only wander but also tear and compare. We can go backward in time or forward. We can wish we had done something else at a certain moment. We can berate ourselves for not having done better or for even double faulting. This, of course, can destroy the love of the game. Expectations are useful to some extent, but when they become pressure-filled, we wish to escape their demands, even to the point of walking off the court or giving up the game altogether.

Gracie does none of this. Occasionally, and very occasionally, she misses the ball Marv throws. She may have not been in the best position to snag it, or her paws may have slipped on the tile floor. Yet, this does not put her off her game at all. She does not worry about what she did wrong. She does not criticize herself. She just gets the ball, gives it to Marv and continues. You never hear her say, "I'm sorry" or "I shouldn't have missed that." You never see her pumping her chest when she catches a difficult toss. There is no ego – no building herself up or putting herself down, just the love of playing the game.

PATIENCE – WHO NEEDS IT?

Tennis is a fast game. Usually you try to hit the ball as hard and fast as you can. You run as fast as you can after it to hit it back even faster. Where does patience come in?

I noticed that Gracie would sit at attention waiting for the next time Marv would toss the ball; she would wait nearly forever.

She could sit with total attentiveness, focus, and patience.

Sometimes on the tennis court we can become impatient. We can become antsy when the server doesn't serve fast enough. We can become eager to end a point before the time is right. We lack patience and are therefore out of "the flow."

Patience is a virtue on and off of the court. To take your time hitting the ball, to take your time tossing the ball up for a serve, to take your time working a point, to take your time gathering games to win a set are hugely important actions to the outcome.

Now, I'm not saying that one should go on in the same manner forever without changing things up. If boredom should set in, change. A little drop shot or a trip to the net can easily alter a monotonous pattern and bring life back into a point.

When patience begins to run out for Gracie, she changes. She changes her strategy. Her intention is still the same: get Marv to toss the ball, but she just uses a different tack.

With Marv reclined on the couch, I observed that Gracie would move from her sitting-at-attention position, take the ball in her mouth, and put it next to his side. He would pretend not to notice; she would nudge it closer to his hand. And if he didn't notice, she would pat his hand with her paw as if to say, *Come on, Marv, let's play. Throw the ball so I can catch it.* He would, of course, oblige. Then, they were off again, playing the game each loved so much.

FORM – WHAT ARE THE BEST STROKES?

One of the most interesting things about Gracie's form in catching balls is that she is flexible.

She has no perfect form that works for every ball, as every ball toss is in reality a little different from the last. She is adaptable. She jumps with her hind legs, but then may have to twist around if the ball is over her back. She does what is necessary to get that ball.

When I learned to play tennis, strokes were exact and rigid. It is not so anymore. Players are far more varied in their stroke production and can alter a basic stroke to fit the occasion, as does Gracie. I applaud this new way, as there is now no standard "right" way to hit the ball. Naturally, having a basic stroke that you can adjust as needed is desirable. Many times I see players who have not had any initial instruction in their tennis strokes and they are limited because of it. They are unable to generate force because of their poor technique. Or, they are unable to toss a ball up to serve in a consistent spot. Even a wrong grip can keep a player from volleying well. I say, "Get some help. Get some instruction."

Naturally, nobody taught Gracie how to jump. She is a self-taught jumping wizard.

ADAPTIBILITY – HOW USEFUL IS IT?

Flexibility in form is one thing; adaptability is another. We players need to adapt to our surroundings whenever and wherever we play. If you are lucky enough to get to play on the grass courts at the All England Club, don't expect the ball to bounce. If you're playing on the red clay at Roland Garros or the Har-Tru courts at the West Side Tennis club at Forrest Hills, don't expect to put the ball away. If you are playing on the hard courts at your local park, don't be surprised if your knees hurt. And, if you ever have a chance to play on the boards at London's Queen's Club, don't expect to see the ball at all.

These are just some of the adaptations a player must make to court surfaces, but then there are the housing and atmospheric adjustments to deal with. Playing in a bubble in Aspen is not the same as playing outdoors in Sydney. The humid air of Florida affects the balls pace as much as the dry weather in La Quinta, California.

Wind, dampness, dryness, and sun all can affect your play. Be adaptable like Gracie. I've seen her play on cloudy days and sunny days. I've seen her slide after a ball on the wood of a basketball court, dig her heels in to chase a ball down on grass, elevate on tile, and rebound magically on sand.

Nothing fazes her. Nothing diverts her from her mission. She adjusts and so can you.

COMPETITION – HOW TO VIEW IT

There are two aspects to competition that I see and Gracie is a master at both.

Occasionally when Ashley and I take Gracie to the park, there are several other dogs in the area. When I wind up and hit the ball half way down the field, the dogs all run after it. One of them gets it; sometimes it's Gracie. Whether she does get it or doesn't get it, she comes back waiting for me to hit it again. As hard as she tries to retrieve the flying ball, she is just as happy when she returns whether she has it or not.

That's the way to play a point: try hard, win or lose, but maintain your inner joy either way. Play for the love of it. You'll play better.

Now, the second part of competition is about the other participant or participants, if you're playing doubles. In the case of Gracie, Marv is the one who is giving her the opportunity to jump for a ball, or me, if I hit it with a racket at the park. That other person is essential to the game she is playing, just as your opponent on the court is essential to you.

Whether that person has a nasty disposition or a pleasant one, while you are playing, that person must be highly valued by you. Without him or her, there is no game, unless you want to hit against a backboard.

Many times I have heard complaints about opponents from other players. "She plays too fast." "I can't trust her calls." "He never keeps score." "He never brings balls."

Never criticize your opponent. Study them. Analyze them, but leave them be and be grateful that person is on the other side of the net. That person makes it possible for you to play.

An opponent stretches you and your abilities by offering up a set of circumstances for you to work with or around. Does that person have a better backhand than forehand? Where is their preferred spot to hit the ball? What about an overhead – is the person capable of putting it away? Can he or she move forward easily?

All of these little observations can go into your head, your own computer and your subconscious, and sort out the best possible ball placement for you at any moment. Play freely and be respectful of your opponent.

The truth is that Gracie is grateful for anyone who will throw her a ball. She's really not picky. Marv and I might think we loom large in her list of favorites, however, if we had no ball in our hands she would drop us for the next pitcher in a second.

INTENSITY – SOMETHING WORTH DEVELOPING

I have never seen as intense a gaze as Gracie's when it comes to tennis balls. If she arrives at our

The Dog That Taught Me Tennis

home without a ball, she goes directly to an entrance table where there are always a couple of used balls. She sits and stares. She stares until someone notices her and gives her a ball.

Once she has a ball in her mouth, she goes directly to Marv, sitting or lying down, and insists that he play. The ball is everything to her at that moment. To her the ball <u>is</u> everything; there is no her. She gives herself no consideration. That's focus. That's intensity.

As you know, we all live in the world of light, provided mainly by our beloved sun. Without light we would not be able to see a thing. When light is controlled, not scattered, and it is greatly compacted, it becomes a laser. It is therefore, highly intense and highly powerful.

That's what you want to be when you are on the tennis court – a laser – unless you're just out for a lark. You want to play with intensity. You want to laser in on the game, on each individual point, on that particular ball. The weather, the viewers, the umpire, if you have one, all play second fiddle to what YOU are doing with the ball. The more you narrow your focus, the more intense and powerful you become.

The moment my mind wanders around when I'm playing a competitive match, I think of Gracie and her extreme dedication to what she is doing, and I'm back in the game. She is a marvel!

FITNESS – HOW IMPORTANT IS IT?

Whether you are planning on playing on the courts at Wimbledon or your local, public parks courts or just go out for a walk, fitness counts. Being in shape is a lifelong challenge. It is a commitment you must make to yourself. No one wants to take care of another or to be taken care of by another, if they have a choice. So, do everyone a favor, especially yourself, and pay attention to that aspect of your life.

It is easy to get sidetracked and put off exercise. It is easier to eat fast food than it is to prepare a home-cooked meal. But in the long run, and I am in the long run, remaining in the best shape you can for the age you are is a good thing.

There is an endless amount of information available to everyone now on the ways and means of remaining healthy. The do's and don'ts are clear. Eat well, drink lots of water, get a good night's sleep, and stay active.

Again, Gracie remains the perfect example of a healthy being. She neither smokes, nor drinks, nor takes drugs. She has great endurance. She runs when running is appropriate, sleeps well, drinks lots of water, and eats only what Ashley gives her.

BEING A CHAMPION – NEVER GIVE UP!

In my experience, I have found that some tennis players play better when they are behind while others play better when they are ahead. Some even quit psychologically when they are losing. Gracie never quits. She plays full out all the time. She knows the secret – she doesn't keep score.

Gracie is a champion in all ways, and you can become one too. Focus your energies toward your goal. Be kind to and respectful of others. Be grateful for the life you have been given. Take care of your health. Live intensely. Play hard and play fair. Love your life and all that is in it and you will be that champion – on and off the court.

For those who wish to increase their ability to concentrate and develop their intuition (useful skills for any tennis player), you may want to practice the following exercise.

A POWERFUL CONCENTRATION EXERCISE

I don't know if Gracie has ever practiced this exercise or not, but I have and it is well worth the effort to do it. It was given to me by a mystic long ago.

It is an Egyptian Yoga exercise that creates new pathways in the brain for more creative thinking. Most of our lives and thinking are ruled by habit, even the tennis we play. By giving energy to new areas, new insights are revealed, greater understanding is achieved, and better strategies evolve. These are just a few of the benefits. The rest are for you to discover.

Although the exercise is apparently simple, the effect can be quite powerful. On the other hand, it is wise to avoid expectations.

This is the first in a series. It is about *clear-sightedness* and will help you see problems more clearly and solve them, whether you are on the court or not. It will also help you focus on the ball with greater ease. I encourage you to jump in. The exercise only takes three minutes. It is best to do it several times a day, prior to meals.

PROPER POSTURE

1. Choose a quiet room where you will not be disturbed, preferably with a simple colored wall.

2. Place a small circle, about the size of a penny, on the wall. I've created one that you can cut out at the back of this book and attach with tape. Or, you may get a felt one at any hardware store.

Place the circle or dot on the wall at exactly eye level when you are seated, and about four to seven feet away from you. During the exercise, "rest" your eyes on this dot without "staring" and without blinking. If there is a source of light in the room, it should be behind you.

3. Sit on a chair with your back straight, not touching the back of the chair. Place your feet flat on the floor, heels about two inches apart, legs and knees open, forming a V shape with the feet and legs.

4. Adjust the height of the chair seat so that your thighs are exactly parallel to the floor and form a right angle to the rest of your body. Straighten your spine, keeping your shoulders slightly pulled back and your chin in.

5. Rest your hands on your thighs, just behind the knees so that the thumbs will point to the inside of the knees, while the fingers, spread open, point to the outside. They should also form a V.

6. Draw your abdomen in gently. Keep your lips lightly closed with your tongue relaxed, resting on the bottom of your mouth, and your teeth slightly parted.

7. Relax every muscle except for those that hold your spine straight.

PREPARATORY BREATH

The purpose of the preparatory breath is to clean the lungs. It consists of a rapid breath made up of short inhalations and expirations through your nose, one after the other without a pause. After seven or eight of these rapid breathing cycles, end with a long and forceful exhalation through your mouth, expelling as completely as possible all the stale air from your lungs.

THE EXERCISE

The exercise is based on the seven-plus-one second rhythm. It would be ideal to use your heartbeats instead of seconds as the units of time. With a little practice you will be able to sense this time interval as a musical beat, without paying much attention to it. **For children**, a five-plus-one second rhythm might be more appropriate.

Check your posture. Make sure you are relaxed. Make the preparatory breath, then "rest" your eyes on the dot, almost as if you are looking through it to infinity.

***

Breathe in for seven seconds (or seven heartbeats), hold your breath for one second, breathe out for seven seconds, keeping the lungs empty for one second. This makes <u>One Breath Cycle</u>. You will do this twelve times.

***

As you inhale, visualize a spiral of "energy" coming into the very center of you clockwise in seven concentric circles. During the exhalation, unwind the spiral counter-clockwise from the center of you outward in seven increasingly larger circles. Do not localize either the very center of yourself or the spiral. Try to "feel" its sweeping movement as you would "feel" a tornado, if you were the atmosphere. Every motion (or energy) in the Universe has the form of a spiral, therefore this visualizing-feeling will attune you to the universal form of motion.

<u>If you blink during the exercise, start over again!</u>

After you have gotten the hang of this part of the exercise and have become fairly familiar with it, and NOT before, you may complete the exercise as follows.

During the first three breath cycles (remember a cycle consists of seven counts in, hold for one, and seven counts out, hold for one) imagine that the dot on the wall is red, while at the same time a red light illuminates the abdomen, sexual area of the body, and the back of the head.

During the next three breath cycles, imagine the dot to become yellow, while at the same time a yellow light bathes your chest area and your forehead.

For the next three cycles, imagine the dot becoming blue (cyan blue) and a blue light illuminating your solar plexus and the top of your head.

Finally, during the last three breaths, imagine the dot becoming white with a brilliant white light illuminating your face, arms and legs.

***

When you have mastered this exercise, you definitely deserve a trophy! Good luck to you! Have fun! The happier you are, the better you play!

Here is another wonderful tennis book by Sally Huss. It is also appropriate for kids as well as adults.

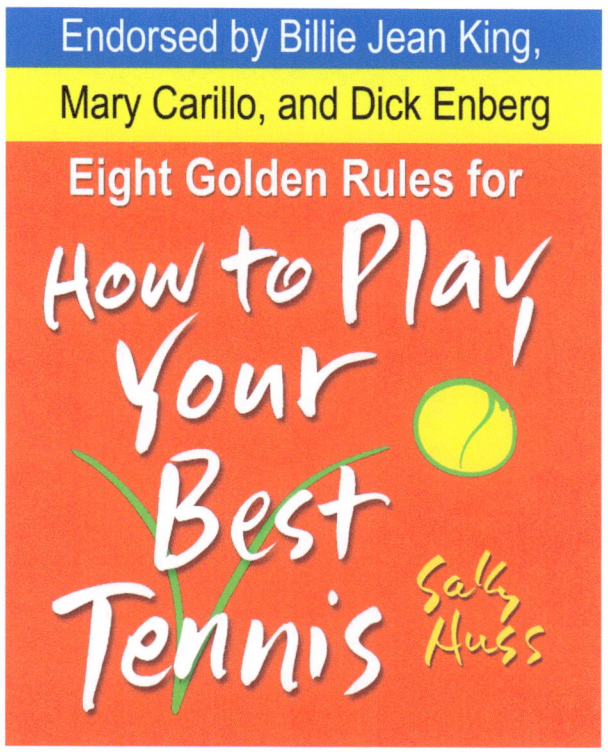

Mary Carillo, CBS and ESPN Sports:
  "Sally Huss has written a simple, sparkling gem of a book. It is wise and gentle, and gives to tennis players what the great UCLA coach John Wooden gave to basketball players with his Pyramid of Success. If you do what Sally suggests you will be more than a better player; you'll be a better person. Perhaps her book should be called *Eight Golden Rules for How To Live Your Best Life.*"

Dick Enberg, CBS and ESPN Sports:

"Loved the book. I've seen Sally Huss play this great game of tennis. She caressed the ball, while fully embracing the experience. Her style and good form are expressed in her *EIGHT GOLDEN RULES FOR HOW TO PLAY YOUR BEST TENNIS*. It's an extension of her proven championship play. The message in her book is direct, kind, respectful, and in its wondrous simplicity, as sharp as a backhand winner down the line. If I were to start playing again, I'd be best served to read this book FIRST and then GRIP a racquet. Game, Set, and Match, Ms. Huss! Oh My!"

Billie Jean King, 39 Grand Slam Titles, Founder of World Team Tennis:

"Tennis is a lifetime sport and fun for players of all ages. In *Eight Golden Rules for How to Play Your Best Tennis*, Sally Huss shows you how to get the most out of your game and how much fun playing tennis can be."

EIGHT GOLDEN RULES FOR HOW TO PLAY YOUR BEST TENNIS may be found on Amazon as an e-book or soft cover book --
http://amzn.com/B004QOAGL4.

Here is a delightful book on ladies league tennis. It too may be found on Amazon as an e-book and in softcover --http://amzn.to/1kI09qs.

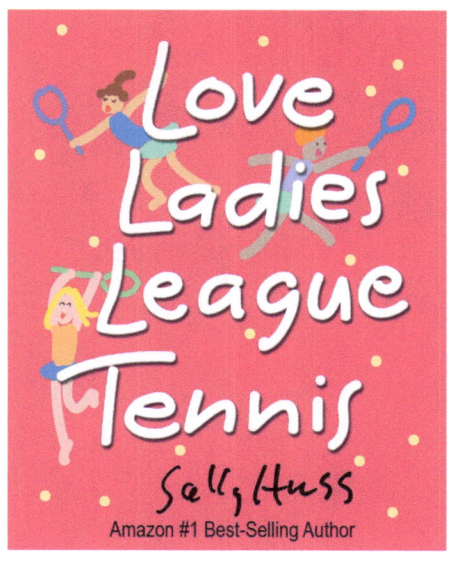

If you liked THE DOG THAT TAUGHT ME TENNIS, please be kind enough to post a short review on Amazon for it.

The adorable children's books of Carol Ann (Ashley) Birtwell may also be found on Amazon.

Sally writes new books all the time. If you would like to be alerted when she has a new book or when one of her books is available as a FREE promotion, just sign up on her website. You'll find a FREE kids' e-book for you too. http://www.sallyhuss.com.

About the Author/Illustrator

Sally Huss

    Sally Huss was a National and Wimbledon Junior Champion, a Wimbledon semi-finalist in singles and doubles, winner of many National senior singles and doubles titles, and still plays ladies league tennis!

    "Bright and happy," "light and whimsical" have been the catch phrases attached to the writings and art of Sally Huss for over 30 years. From inspirational books, children's books to her King Features syndicated newspaper panel "Happy Musings," all of her creations are happy in nature and free-spirited in style.

Sally is a graduate of USC with a degree in Fine Art and through the years has had 26 of her own licensed art galleries throughout the world.

THE DOG THAT TAUGHT ME TENNIS
By Sally Huss
Copyright 2016 Sally Huss Inc.
Huss Publishing

No part of this publication may be reproduced, sold, stored in a retrieval system, or transmitted in any form, or by any means (electronic, mechanical, photocopying, resending or otherwise) without permission by the author.

www.ingramcontent.com/pod-product-compliance
Lightning Source LLC
Chambersburg PA
CBHW042218050426
42453CB00001BA/9